How THE WIDOW

WON THE DEACON

William James Lampton

[ZHINGOORA BOOKS]

HOW THE WIDOW WON THE DEACON

Of course the Widow Stimson never tried to win Deacon Hawkins, nor any other man, for that matter. A widow doesn't have to try to win a man; she wins without trying. Still, the Widow Stimson sometimes wondered why the deacon was so blind as not to see how her fine farm adjoining his equally fine place on the outskirts of the town might not be brought under one management with mutual benefit to both parties at interest. Which one that management might become was a matter of future detail. The widow knew how to run a farm successfully, and a large farm is not much more difficult to run than one of half the size. She had also had one husband, and knew something more than running a farm successfully. Of all of which the deacon was perfectly well aware, and still he had not been moved by the merging spirit of the age to propose consolidation.

This interesting situation was up for discussion at the Wednesday afternoon meeting of the Sisters' Sewing Society.

"For my part," Sister Susan Spicer, wife of the Methodist minister, remarked as she took another tuck in a fourteen-year-old girl's skirt for a ten-year-old—"for my part, I can't see why Deacon Hawkins and Kate Stimson don't see the error of their ways and depart from them."

"I rather guess *she* has," smiled Sister Poteet, the grocer's better half, who had taken an afternoon off from the store in order to be present.

"Or is willing to," added Sister Maria Cartridge, a spinster still possessing faith, hope, and charity, notwithstanding she had been on the waiting list a long time.

"Really, now," exclaimed little Sister Green, the doctor's wife, "do you think it is the deacon who needs urging?"

"It looks that way to me," Sister Poteet did not hesitate to affirm.

"Well, I heard Sister Clark say that she had heard him call her 'Kitty' one night when they were eating ice-cream at the Mite

Society," Sister Candish, the druggist's wife, added to the fund of reliable information on hand.

"'Kitty,' indeed!" protested Sister Spicer. "The idea of anybody calling Kate Stimson 'Kitty'! The deacon will talk that way to 'most any woman, but if she let him say it to her more than once, she must be getting mighty anxious, I think."

"Oh," Sister Candish hastened to explain, "Sister Clark didn't say she had heard him say it twice.'"

"Well, I don't think she heard him say it once," Sister Spicer asserted with confidence.

"I don't know about that," Sister Poteet argued. "From all I can see and hear I think Kate Stimson wouldn't object to 'most anything the deacon would say to her, knowing as she does that he ain't going to say anything he shouldn't say."

"And isn't saying what he should," added Sister Green, with a sly snicker, which went around the room softly.

"But as I was saying—" Sister Spicer began, when Sister Poteet, whose rocker, near the window, commanded a view of the front gate, interrupted with a warning, "'Sh-'sh."

"Why shouldn't I say what I wanted to when—" Sister Spicer began.

"There she comes now," explained Sister Poteet, "and as I live the deacon drove her here in his sleigh, and he's waiting while she comes in. I wonder what next," and Sister Poteet, in conjunction with the entire society, gasped and held their eager breaths, awaiting the entrance of the subject of conversation.

Sister Spicer went to the front door to let her in, and she was greeted with the greatest cordiality by everybody.

"We were just talking about you and wondering why you were so late coming," cried Sister Poteet. "Now take off your things and make up for lost time. There's a pair of pants over there to be cut down to fit that poor little Snithers boy."

The excitement and curiosity of the society were almost more than could be borne, but never a sister let on that she knew the deacon was at the gate waiting. Indeed, as far as the widow could discover, there was not the slightest indication that anybody had ever heard there was such a person as the deacon in existence.

"Oh," she chirruped, in the liveliest of humors, "you will have to excuse me for today. Deacon Hawkins overtook me on the way here, and here said I had simply got to go sleigh-riding with him. He's waiting out at the gate now."

"Is that so?" exclaimed the society unanimously, and rushed to the window to see if it were really true.

"Well, did you ever?" commented Sister Poteet, generally.

"Hardly ever," laughed the widow, good-naturedly, "and I don't want to lose the chance. You know Deacon Hawkins isn't asking somebody every day to go sleighing with him. I told him I'd go if he would bring me around here to let you know what had become of me, and so he did. Now, good-by, and I'll be sure to be present at the next meeting. I have to hurry because he'll get fidgety."

The widow ran away like a lively schoolgirl. All the sisters watched her get into the sleigh with the deacon, and resumed the previous discussion with greatly increased interest.

But little recked the widow and less recked the deacon. He had bought a new horse and he wanted the widow's opinion of it, for the Widow Stimson was a competent judge of fine horseflesh. If Deacon Hawkins had one insatiable ambition it was to own a horse which could fling its heels in the face of the best that Squire Hopkins drove. In his early manhood the deacon was no deacon by a great deal. But as the years gathered in behind him he put off most of the frivolities of youth and held now only to the one of driving a fast horse. No other man in the county drove anything faster except Squire Hopkins, and him the deacon had not been able to throw the dust over. The deacon would get good ones, but somehow never could he find one that the squire didn't get a better. The squire had also in the early days beaten the deacon in the race for a certain pretty girl he dreamed about. But the girl and the squire had lived happily ever after and the deacon, being a philosopher, might have forgotten the squire's superiority had it been manifested in this one regard only. But in horses, too—that graveled the deacon.

"How much did you give for him?" was the widow's first query, after they had reached a stretch of road that was good going and the deacon had let him out for a length or two.

"Well, what do you suppose? You're a judge."

"More than I would give, I'll bet a cookie."

"Not if you was as anxious as I am to show Hopkins that he can't drive by everything on the pike."

"I thought you loved a good horse because he was a good horse," said the widow, rather disapprovingly.

"I do, but I could love him a good deal harder if he would stay in front of Hopkins's best."

"Does he know you've got this one?"

"Yes, and he's been blowing round town that he is waiting to pick me up on the road some day and make my five hundred dollars look like a pewter quarter."

"So you gave five hundred dollars for him, did you?" laughed the widow.

"Is it too much?"

"Um-er," hesitated the widow, glancing along the graceful lines of the powerful trotter, "I suppose not if you can beat the squire."

"Right you are," crowed the deacon, "and I'll show him a thing or two in getting over the ground," he added with swelling pride.

"Well, I hope he won't be out looking for you today, with me in your sleigh," said the widow, almost apprehensively, "because, you know, deacon, I have always wanted you to beat Squire Hopkins."

The deacon looked at her sharply. There was a softness in her tones that appealed to him, even if she had not expressed such agreeable sentiments. Just what the deacon might have said or done after the impulse had been set going must remain unknown, for at the crucial moment a sound of militant bells, bells of defiance, jangled up behind them, disturbing their personal absorption, and they looked around simultaneously. Behind the bells was the squire in his sleigh drawn by his fastest stepper, and he was alone, as the deacon was not. The widow weighed one hundred and sixty pounds, net—which is weighting a horse in a race rather more than the law allows.

But the deacon never thought of that. Forgetting everything except his cherished ambition, he braced himself for the contest, took a twist hold on the lines, sent a sharp, quick call to his horse, and let him out for all that was in him. The squire followed suit and the deacon. The road was wide and the snow was worn down smooth. The track couldn't have been in better condition. The Hopkins colors were not five rods behind the Hawkins colors as they got away. For half a mile it was nip and tuck, the deacon encouraging his horse and the widow encouraging the deacon, and then the squire began creeping up. The deacon's horse was a good one, but he was not accustomed to hauling freight in a race. A half-mile of it was as much as he could stand, and he weakened under the strain.

Not handicapped, the squire's horse forged ahead, and as his nose pushed up to the dashboard of the deacon's sleigh, that good man groaned in agonized disappointment and bitterness of spirit. The widow was mad all over that Squire Hopkins should take such a mean advantage of his rival. Why didn't he wait till another time when the deacon was alone, as he was? If she had her way she never would, speak to Squire Hopkins again, nor to his wife, either. But her resentment was not helping the deacon's horse to win.

Slowly the squire pulled closer to the front; the deacon's horse, realizing what it meant to his master and to him, spurted bravely, but, struggle as gamely as he might, the odds were too many for him, and he dropped to the rear. The squire shouted in triumph as he drew past the deacon, and the dejected Hawkins shrivelled into a heap on the seat, with only his hands sufficiently alive to hold the lines. He had been beaten again, humiliated before a woman, and that, too, with the best horse that he could hope to put against the ever-conquering squire. Here sank his fondest hopes, here ended his ambition. From this on he would drive a mule or an automobile. The fruit of his desire had turned to ashes in his mouth.

But no. What of the widow? She realized, if the deacon did not, that she, not the squire's horse, had beaten the deacon's, and she was ready to make what atonement she could. As the squire passed ahead of the deacon she was stirred by a noble resolve. A deep bed of drifted snow lay close by the side of the road not far in front. It was soft and safe and she smiled as she looked at it as though waiting for her. Without a hint of her purpose, or a sign to disturb the deacon in his final throes, she rose as the sleigh ran near its edge, and with a spring which had many a time sent her lightly from the ground to the bare back of a horse in the meadow, she cleared the robes and lit plump in the drift. The deacon's horse knew before the deacon did that something had happened in his favor, and was quick to respond. With his first jump of relief the deacon suddenly revived, his hopes came fast again, his blood retingled, he gathered himself, and, cracking his lines, he shot forward, and three minutes later he had passed the squire as though he were hitched to the fence. For a quarter of a mile the squire made heroic efforts to recover his vanished prestige, but effort was useless, and finally concluding that he was practically left standing, he veered off from the main road down a farm lane to find some spot in which to hide the humiliation of his defeat. The deacon, still going at a clipping gait, had one eye over his shoulder as wary drivers always have on such occasions, and when he saw the squire was off the track he slowed down and jogged along with the apparent intention of continuing indefinitely. Presently an idea struck him, and he looked around for the widow. She was not where he had seen her last. Where was she? In the enthusiasm of victory he had forgotten her. He was so dejected at the moment she had leaped that he did not realize what she had done, and two minutes later he was so elated that, shame on him! he did not care. With her, all was lost; without her, all was won, and the deacon's greatest ambition was to win. But now, with victory perched on his horse-collar, success his at last, he thought of the widow, and he did care. He cared so much that he almost threw his horse off his feet by the abrupt turn he gave him, and back down the pike he flew as if a legion of squires were after him.

He did not know what injury she might have sustained; She might have been seriously hurt, if not actually killed. And why? Simply to make it possible for him to win. The deacon shivered as he thought of it, and urged his horse to greater speed. The squire, down the lane, saw him whizzing along and accepted it profanely as an exhibition for his especial benefit. The deacon now had forgotten the squire as he had only so shortly before forgotten the widow. Two hundred yards from the drift into which she had jumped there was a turn in the road, where some trees shut off the sight, and the deacon's anxiety increased momentarily until he reached this point. From here he could see ahead, and down there in the middle of the road stood the widow waving her shawl as a banner of triumph, though she could only guess at results. The deacon came on with a rush, and pulled up alongside of her in a condition of nervousness he didn't think possible to him.

"Hooray! hooray!" shouted the widow, tossing her shawl into the air. "You beat him. I know you did. Didn't you? I saw you pulling ahead at the turn yonder. Where is he and his old plug?"

"Oh, bother take him and his horse and the race and everything. Are you hurt?" gasped the deacon, jumping out, but mindful to keep the lines in his hand. "Are you hurt?" he repeated, anxiously, though she looked anything but a hurt woman.

"If I am," she chirped, cheerily, "I'm not hurt half as bad as I would have been if the squire had beat you, deacon. Now don't you worry about me. Let's hurry back to town so the squire won't get another chance, with no place for me to jump."

And the deacon? Well, well, with the lines in the crook of his elbow the deacon held out his arms to the widow and——. The sisters at the next meeting of the Sewing Society were unanimously of the opinion that any woman who would risk her life like that for a husband was mighty anxious.

End of the book.

www.ingramcontent.com/pod-product-compliance
Lightning Source LLC
Chambersburg PA
CBHW060022300526
45794CB00003B/1265